Things are not where they should be.

Jasmine Tran, grade 2

Christina Fullenkamp, grade 8

The Storm

Students of Biloxi, Mississippi, Remember Hurricane Katrina

COMPILED BY
Barbara Barbieri McGrath

Charlesbridge

To My Friends at St. Peter School —

Celebrate humanity!

Join in!

♥ BBMcGrath

2008

Introduction

It was hard to believe what I was seeing. I thought, "How can wind bend metal and destroy brick buildings?"

W. Louis McGrath, Massachusetts college student

Shortly after Hurricane Katrina devastated the Gulf Coast, I listened to a newscast reporting that a school had reopened. I immediately thought, "No way!" From the pictures the media was showing, it didn't even look like people could live there. How could children be going back to school?

A few phone calls later, I found out it was true. As a children's book author, I visit schools nationwide, and so I thought maybe I could help by traveling to damaged areas to entertain the children and give their teachers a little break. I called Brent Farmer at Charlesbridge Publishing and asked him to sponsor my trip. He did so gladly and also offered cases of books to donate. That got me thinking that the students in my hometown of Natick, Massachusetts, could also send a few books to help restock classrooms. That effort was called Books for Biloxi. With the help of the entire community, thousands of books were collected, packed, and sent—first to the sheriff's office in Hattiesburg, and when UPS could get through, to the Biloxi Public Schools directly.

I went to the Gulf Coast with my son, Louis, and delivered some of the books personally. We met Nancy Hunter, an instructional trainer for Biloxi Public Schools. She told us that our books were the only ones the schools would have when they reopened. To her delight, books kept on arriving long after I returned home.

No one can live through something as uncontrollable and destructive as Katrina and not be changed in some way. I got the idea for putting this book together when a teacher reminded me that one of the most important ways children heal is through the arts. That thought stayed with me, and with Nancy Hunter's help, the work of compiling and selecting began. This very personal collection of drawings, paintings, and writings from Biloxi's children is both heart wrenching and life affirming in its honesty. I'm very honored to be able to share it with you today.

Barbara Barbieri McGrath
Natick, Massachusetts
July 2006

5

Evacuation

We traveled all the way to Missouri. It was a very long trip, and I miss my home in Mississippi.

Patience Wells, grade 3

Ian Cowell, grade 3

Biloxi High is always used as a "special needs" shelter during hurricanes. The local civil defense folks and emergency medical response teams will set up a wing in my halls to take care of the elderly and ill. My family and I stay there, also, to assist. During and after Katrina, however, I ended up with approximately 800 evacuees, the Federal Disaster Medical Assistance Team, Federal Protective Services, Red Cross, state militia, and a full-blown medical clinic complete with helicopter "med-evacs" in the parking lot. Needless to say, there are lots of stories to tell now, including the wedding of two evacuees.

Pamela Manners, principal

Before Katrina we had to do a lot in a very short time. We had to put the dog in a room. Next we helped my aunt Stevonne get her house in order. We gathered ice, water, noodles, eggs, cheese, bread, chips, air freshener, disinfectant spray, gas, batteries, candles, flashlights, baby wipes, and other supplies. Next we went to my aunt De-de's house in Ocean Springs and cooked and waited for Katrina to come.

Arnessa Smallman, grade 5

A few days before Katrina it was very calm, and so was the water. We went to the store and stocked up enough food for at least a month. We went to my uncle's house, and we had a lot of fun. We went to sleep, woke up, and watched movies all day. We went to sleep, and the next morning we woke up and the house was rocking. We sat on the inside porch and watched my uncle's neighbors' house fall.

Matthew Santiago, grade 5

Rodrick Murphy, grade 2

"Lost Shrimp Boat,"
Anthony Demoran, kindergarten

One day when I got home from school I put the news on TV, and it said a storm was coming. The name of the storm was Katrina! My mom said that we had to leave before the hurricane. My mom was scared. So we went to my aunt's house. We brought tons of food. We had a generator, and the power went off and on. I slept with no electricity.

Jennifer Kelly, grade 3

On my shrimp boat, we had everything we needed to get ready to go away from Biloxi. My whole family was on the boat, except my two oldest brothers, who were going to Texas. All of the tree's branches broke in half and flew across the ocean. My family was scared, and we thought we were going to die. During the hurricane, the rope that holds all the boats together broke, and all the boats started to move back because the wind was so strong. Some boats flew across the ocean, and the people who were in the boats died.

Nancy Nguyen, grade 5

When The storm came we mom Dad, I brother I sister stayed in the boat. It was my mom and dad and my brother and sister and me. The wind and rain was all day.

Jonathan Tran, grade 1

Sze-Wing Cheung, grade 3

My family and I left Biloxi on August 28, 2005. There were only 24 hours left until Hurricane Katrina made landfall. We decided to go to Panama City, Florida, and stay at a hotel until the powerful hurricane died. Panama City, Florida, was affected by Hurricane Katrina, but not as badly as Biloxi. The next day was horrible because Hurricane Katrina made landfall.

Kenny Dinh, grade 6

I got about three hours of sleep before I was woken up by my mom because the winds were getting bad. So it was five a.m., and my mom made eggs, biscuits, and grits, also some oranges (kind of like our "last supper"). Right after (and I mean my last mouthful) I finished eating, the power went out.

Jennifer Weiss, grade 8

Huyen Nguyen, grade 1

Storm

A morning of thunder
A morning of rain
A morning of sorrow
A morning of pain

Jasmine Ray, grade 8

Zaneta Whatley Montgomery, grade 4

It brings tears to my eyes, even now, when I think of those people being driven in by military transport vehicles and herded up to my hallway—no shoes, all wet, many without shirts, and most in pajamas. But the most painful thing was hearing, "Miss Manners!" and seeing two of my students, drenched and shaking, being moved in with all the rest. What was once a faceless storm all of a sudden became personal.

Tracy Manners Campbell,
English teacher

August 29, 2005, was the worst day ever! First, siding was flying everywhere. Shingles were falling like pancakes. Everything got peeled like an orange inside and outside. There were very strong winds, and the rain was horrible. My family were the only people in the neighborhood. My grandparents and my family stayed in our living room. My sister's ceiling came down. It was scary.

Beatriz Cruz, grade 3

I asked my mom, "Is that a train? Why is a train running down the tracks during Katrina?" My mom answered, "Tonysha, that's not a train. That's Katrina!" All a sudden the ceiling caved in. Everyone started screaming, and the babies were crying!

Tonysha Hawthorne, grade 3

Beatriz Cruz, grade 3

Elijah Allen, grade 2

When I saw all that water I started to cry.

Wendy Smith, grade 6

We had a mini-TV and watched the news on WLOX. One thing you need to know is that water started coming in our house a lot. Then everybody went upstairs and into two rooms.

During Hurricane Katrina we heard things tapping on the windows. We heard windows breaking downstairs and things floating all around the house. Things started floating out of the house. While all of that was happening my grandpa was snapping pictures of the water inside and outside our house.

Britney Steel, grade 5

Robbie Cornelson, grade 3

Cathy Tran, grade 2

The first instant we knew we were all in trouble was when we saw that tidal wave come through to the Back Bay and hit us with such a force, it almost smashed all the windows. Immediately, water started to flood in. In another half an hour, water was up to almost my hips. In another half an hour, though, the water started to creep out of the apartment. This water ruined everything it touched.

That wind was so strong that a whole building fell apart in front of my face in at least one hour. It tore shingles off and pulled a car into a lake that was in the middle of the apartment complex. The whole time I was sitting on the cabinet top just watching for it all to be over with. It was freaking everyone out. My dad had even said that if the water had gotten as high as his head, then he would have had to get a mattress, and we all would have had to go onto the second floor and hope it wouldn't get any higher. Everyone just wanted it to end.

I think that from now on, we will always leave town. This storm took a little bit too much out of us.

Kirstie Romero, grade 8

Thong Tra, grade 1

A 90 foot wave hit my house!

Tyler Lee, grade 1

When the water got high, I saw houses falling and cars floating. Then my mom heard someone screaming. It was a lady with her kids, and we saved them by pulling them up by sheets that my aunt had. Then we saw another lady, and she was swimming and was about to panic. We told her not to panic and helped her up the stairs.

Michael Morrissette, grade 6

"My Family in the Storm," Justus Toliver, grade 4

Cassandra Sanders, grade 3

I looked outside and saw that the trees were moving back and forth, like a flexible ruler. A couple of hours later, the adults saw that some of the boats outside had gotten loose from the trees and started to sail away. The adults were crying and praying, hoping that everyone would survive the hurricane. They prayed that the ropes wouldn't break loose and make our boat sail away.

Kim Tran, grade 6

Tai Nguyen, grade 2

James Donitzen, grade 5

During the storm the water started coming in our house. My dad tried to save some things but the water was coming in too fast. The water reached eight feet in our house. We held hands and prayed and asked God to let the water go down. The wind was very strong and we thought the roof was going to come off. We were calling people on their cell phones during the storm to check on them.

Jarred Strickland, grade 5

Carmelita Davis, grade 9

My roof flew off the house

Adarius McCormick, kindergarten

During the hurricane, I was in my house in the attic. My family and I watched with our own eyes as the water kept rising. What transpired is that everything in our house began to float! The water was about six or seven feet high in our house. We were hoping that the water would stop rising. My sisters and I started to pray quietly. Then, suddenly, the water stopped rising. We were very happy that the water paused and started to go downward. When the house dried, we started to climb down out of the attic. Everything in my house was ruined!

Hang Nguyen, grade 6

Viet Tran, grade 3

Hoang Pham, grade 3

Then the water moved to the stairs. And then me and my sister Tamia got scared and started to cry and cried for a long time. Also, my mother cried because she didn't like to see us cry.

Zimyre Redmon, grade 4

Thuy-Vi Le, grade 3

Mariah Sullivan, kindergarten

I thought Katrina was going to turn around, but she came right in and hit Mississippi. I'm sad because I had to swim from my house to two different houses. I had to go to the biggest house on the street. Then when we got there we had to put some dry clothes on.

Lucas Evans, grade 6

Diana Nguyen, grade 1

Christian Davis, grade 2

On the day of the hurricane I stayed at a church. The wind was blowing very hard, and the water kept rising. When the water got to about thirty feet I prayed to God that everything would be alright. I stayed at the church for about another day, and the next day I went outside and saw everything was gone. That hurricane really woke a lot of people up and made them realize life is too short.

Ricketta McDonald, grade 6

Artist unknown

Aftermath

My house drowned.

Vy Pham, kindergarten

Sharoon Cruz, grade 8

Justin Pounds, grade 4

After the storm was over, my family went home and looked at what had happened to our house. Once we got there, there was mud everywhere, and it smelled like rotten eggs! Our windows were busted out. Our furniture was gone, and my favorite chair, that I used to sit in, was *stuck* in the ceiling!

Prentice Jackson, grade 6

After the storm I was extremely surprised at what I witnessed. Our house moved and flooded. Our beds, drawers, furniture, telephones, and clothes were everywhere. Our computers were stolen. Now I live in a FEMA trailer that is in front of my flooded house. I felt hurt and positively horrible. Certainly, this occurrence was extremely dangerous and devastating.

Kimberly Bui, grade 5

Biloxi-Ocean Springs Bridge

Rian Walker, grade 5

39

Jonathan Trinh, grade 3

After the storm, I returned to Biloxi and found my home broken in two and leaning to the left.

Ro'Darius Woulard, grade 6

AfterMath of Hurricane Katrina

Tabbetha Denley, grade 8

Matthew Santiago, grade 5

After not being able to take showers for a while, I began to get sores in my hair. My head itched and hurt. And having heat rashes made it uncomfortable to do anything. Once we were able to shower, we used a hose. And even then, it was only every other day. So I had to try to wash off the stench and sores with the ice-cold water. Going to the bathroom in a plastic bag made our life before seem like a luxury.

Everything in life is a privilege, not a right. And I never believed that until I lost it all.

Melissa Woodruff, grade 11

My sister stayed in her apartment in Hattiesburg, and we couldn't get in touch with her to make sure she was OK. So my mom kept saying, "I am going to go to Hattiesburg to make sure my baby is OK, and the police can't stop me," because the police were turning people around and telling them the roads were too dangerous to be on. My dad and I actually had to lock my mom in the bedroom just to keep her off the roads.

Katie Nicole Varnado, grade 6

Esteban Selva-Castillo, grade 9

43

Chance Keenon, grade 5

Before Katrina we got to have hot lunches. There were enough chocolate milks to go around. All of my friends were here. We were able to play lots of stuff. Now we have cold lunches. There are not enough chocolate milks to go around. Most of my friends are not here. Some of the gym equipment is gone.

Bobby Scott, grade 4

We now live in a FEMA trailer. It is small and very crowded. I really do wish that everything was back to normal. I also miss my house. Then at other times I think, why did this happen? Did we do something wrong? Sometimes, I lie in the dark thinking about this, but other times when I wake up, I feel happy that I'm still alive.

Nikki Tran, grade 6

My mom was sad because a friend's mom asked us to take her dog, but we didn't and now he's dead. My dad is having a hard time because of what he saw after the storm. All he does is go to work, come home, and sleep. I hope people can recover from the devastation of this storm and all the hard times they have been through.

Andy Latimer, grade 5

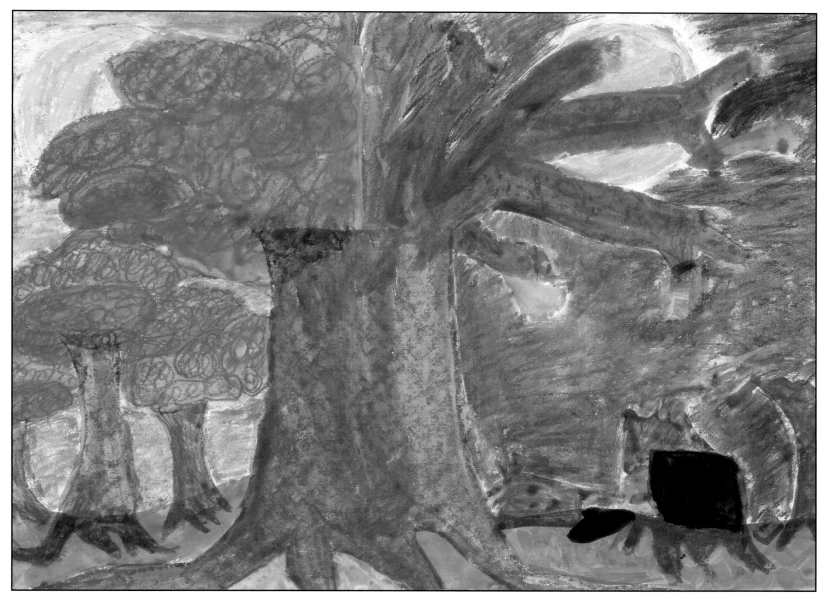

"Before and After," Angelica Alderman, grade 8

Crystal Kokubun, grade 4

That first day back in school was a day for children to talk if they wanted to, or just listen if that was their wish. The children, traumatized by Katrina, spoke in whispers as if they were still in fear of some new danger. The girls were eager to share their Katrina stories. More of the boys kept their feelings to themselves. Eric, a third-grade Vietnamese child, asked me if I could please answer a question for him. His voice was barely a whisper, and I had to get right next to him to hear the question. His face told me it was a very important question, and he was desperate for an answer.

He whispered, "Mrs. Lawrence, what is the 'state of emergency'?" Radio and TV had bombarded the Coast for weeks with, "We are in a state of emergency." Poor Eric must have felt like Dorothy in *The Wizard of Oz*, only he had no magic red shoes to click.

Deborah Lawrence, art teacher

When we came home I was devastated to see what happened to our house. It got tossed around like a beach ball on the waves. I learned that when you run from a storm, you should take your favorite things with you, or they might end up like the beach ball—lost forever.

Erica Davidson, grade 4

Walking back to the church, I found my friend. She was with some of her family, but something was wrong. I noticed her mother wasn't with them. Then her brother said to me, "Don't ask where my mother is." He started telling me that he tried to save her, but she went under the water. I started to cry as I listened to what he told me. A couple of days later, they found my friend's mother under her two-story house.

Brittany Gines, grade 6

Ashley Johnson, grade 8

47

Thirty-five years from now I will have something to tell my children and their children. I will tell them that I lived through Katrina. That's Hurricane Katrina. This storm was devastating. So many dead bodies are on the coast. You can smell the stench in the air. Katrina didn't let anything get in her way.

While we were at the navy base they had prayer meeting and a lady said, "Pray for my husband. Make sure he is alright." The next day she saw her house on the news. The news reporter said, "During Katrina's hard winds this house was flattened to the ground. We found one body in it." Tears rolled down the lady's face. "That's my husband!" she cried.

I felt so melancholy. I started shooting waterworks. It was incredibly sad. Although I may feel sadness over me, I am so blessed to live. To me what counts the most is that my family and I lived through Katrina.

Triston Rodgers, grade 6

Darlena Vo, grade 8

49

Hope

The lighthouse was built in 1848 and is 158 years old. It is 65 feet tall and made out of cast iron. The lighthouse is a symbol of strength for Biloxi.

River Broussard, grade 4

Chris Fury, grade 4

Trey Rodolfich, grade 4

Zachary Parker, grade 4

Marquis Harriel, grade 4

Zimyre Redmon, grade 4

Erica Davidson, grade 4

Mackenzie Hunt, grade 4

Seven months later, my family is doing great! We all have new clothes and shoes. Our house is almost done. People came from all over the world to help us. We are going to be moving out of our trailer in a couple of months. I'm so glad that we will finally be in a house!

D'Laura Shelby, grade 6

When we got home, the storm was over. Trash was everywhere. My brother, mom, and I walked around the neighborhood to see what we could salvage. I found a magnolia flower.

Tyler Reeve, grade 6

For the first time I could remember, my sister and I got along.

Aaron Massey, grade 6

Sarah Fake, grade 6

And Then the Morning Came

The heavens spun in darkness,
The sky of darkest gray.
The whole earth shook around us,
And then the morning came.

The people moved in silence.
No life-light could be found.
And in the gleaming moonlight,
The waves came crashing down.

And then a shaking thunder,
A tidal surge had come.
The roads became as paper,
And then we saw the sun.

All became silent.
No moving tongues were heard.
We gazed into the heavens,
The morning had finally come.

Ashley Warr, grade 11

"Katrina Bird," Harley Wilson, grade 2

Every school district has been adopted by multiple schools, individuals, and civic groups from places as far away as New Jersey, Washington, and California. We have received several donations from Canada. Not only was the number of donations impressive, but the magnitude of some of the assistance was beyond anything that I could have imagined.

I'll never again take the same view of how people in other areas are struggling after a catastrophe. Hurricane Katrina exceeded all of my expectations about what a tropical cyclone can do to an area. But while the storm's destruction was distressing, the totally unexpected response of these amazing people who chose to offer assistance to our struggling community has provided more positive energy than any destruction Katrina could ever have produced.

Dr. Tim Havard, Director of Administrative Services

Now I am excited. My family is doing great. I'm about to move back into my house. People from everywhere across the United States were helping with my house. If I was older and had a job, I would give them lots of money. I thank them very, very, very much for helping my family. I'm happy that it is all over now.

Brittany Gines, grade 6

Thanks for helping us.

Leonard Williams, grade 1

Never a Goodbye

As I walked past my house in ruins
And stood in the middle of Highway 90,
The long road was empty,
And no cars, no trucks, were flying by me.

I remembered how our city used to be
Before the day that changed history.
There was so much on that stretch of land
That stood between me and the sea.

Some fled and some stayed.
Katrina came and then went.
We saw our lives destroyed in pieces,
But our spirits were not broken, only bent.

I have faith in my city and state.
I know we will rebuild stronger.
We will make our big comeback
And survive and thrive even longer.

The time it will take until then
Will seem to last forever,
But the courage and strength we now have
Will make us only much better.

Trial and tribulation take a toll,
But our hopes will never die.
Our state, our country, the world will know—
Never will Biloxi say goodbye.

Saunders Johansen, grade 12

Artist unknown

Nathaniel Morrow, grade 2

Hurricane Katrina has changed me. I'm like a whole new person. I see things differently. I learned to love something while you have it. My neighborhood didn't make it. My house got four feet of water. I was mad at first. Then I thought it could be a new beginning.

Danielle Johnson, grade 6

My family and I are doing the best we can do right now. We are grateful for everything people have given us. I am blessed for having a trailer, water, and electricity. My dad got his job functional again, but my mother is without a job. My brothers, sisters, and I are in school right now. That is fantastic! I have been learning as much as possible.

Jerry Truong, grade 6

Each day things get better, but we know it will take a long time to be back to a normal way of life.

Jarred Strickland, grade 5

Artist unknown

Afterword

Most kids are relatively resilient—some more than others—and without that resilience I'm not sure if we'd ever learn to cope with life and the attendant trauma that goes with it as we grow up.

Dr. Paul Tisdale, superintendent

Low tide reveals prone trees protruding from the sandy Gulf floor. To me they are symbolic of what Biloxi lost in the storm: historic buildings, homes, two brand-new schools, and most devastatingly, fifty-two lives. In addition, twenty-six percent of our student population relocated elsewhere. It is unsettling to the students that some of their friends evacuated and then disappeared. During our low-tide moments our losses are evident and still raw.

While we are busy and unaware of it, the tide creeps back in and things appear normal. On the surface, Biloxi is recovering. Each week additional businesses are able to reopen, and the economy is beginning to rebound. Slowly but surely homes are being restored. Both Nichols and Gorenflo Elementary Schools will reopen in January 2007.

I could not be more proud of the teachers of the Biloxi Public Schools for their unwavering commitment to provide the best school year for our students after the storm. It never occurred to us to ask for help, and we were overwhelmed at the unsolicited response from others. We learned that compassion coupled with action is a powerful combination. For the help we have received, we will be forever grateful.

Whether we have been here for generations or for only a year, most of us will do whatever it takes to remain here. We may live in a FEMA camper, live with in-laws, repair what was left by the storm, rebuild on the same slab, or even relocate to another piece of property, but we will remain residents of the Mississippi Gulf Coast. Why? It is sacred ground. It is home.

Nancy Hunter, Instructional Trainer, Biloxi Public Schools
July 2006

Jyquez Dubose, kindergarten

To the Biloxi Public Schools and their dedication to excellence in education—B. B. M.

Published by Charlesbridge
85 Main Street
Watertown, MA 02472
(617) 926-0329
www.charlesbridge.com

Library of Congress Cataloging-in-Publication Data is available upon request.
   ISBN-13: 978-1-58089-172-1 (reinforced for library use)
   ISBN-10: 1-58089-172-1 (reinforced for library use)
   ISBN-13: 978-1-58089-173-8 (softcover)
   ISBN-10: 1-58089-173-X (softcover)

Printed in the United States of America
(hc) 10 9 8 7 6 5 4 3 2 1
(sc) 10 9 8 7 6 5 4 3 2 1

Display type set in Nuevo Litho, designed by David
   Bergsland, and text type set in Adobe Caslon
Color separations by Chroma Graphics, Singapore
Printed and bound by Lake Book Maufacturing, Inc.
Production supervision by Brian G. Walker
Designed by Susan Mallory Sherman

The author and publisher have made every effort to secure permission to use the names and work of the students featured herein. In some cases, however, we have been unable to locate the creators of the text or art. We will be happy to include corrected credits in future printings of the book.

Acknowledgments

This book could not have happened without the help and hard work of Nancy Hunter, instructional trainer from Biloxi; Yolanda LeRoy, a talented editorial director; Susan Sherman, a brilliant art director; Alyssa Mito Pusey, a diligent managing editor; and an energetic publishing team at Charlesbridge. Thanks to all of you. I would also like to thank Brent Farmer, president and publisher of Charlesbridge, for his generosity in sponsoring my trip to Biloxi and for his support of this endeavor.

I would like to acknowledge the generosity of the students, extended community, and businesses in Natick, Massachusetts, who in an incredibly short amount of time collected, packed, and shipped thousands of books to the Biloxi Public Schools.

Hugs to my husband, Will, for his encouragement; to my son, Louis, for making children laugh with his music (it was a pleasure traveling with you); and to my daughter, Emily, for her artistic advice.

When Dr. Tisdale, superintendent of Biloxi Public Schools, announced that schools would reopen after the hurricane, he told his staff that the conditions and emotional issues wouldn't be good, but the one thing that *would* be good was the education. Biloxi's students are lucky to be taught by the following teachers, all of whom took the time to encourage their students to send in submissions for this book: Elesia Adkins, Alicia Blair, Shawn Bolton, Lisa Bouvette, Tracy Manners Campbell, Dee Fury, Tricia Goyette, Stacey Hales, Perry Howard, Dawn Jacobs, Laurie Johnston, Nancy Lamey, Deborah Lawrence, James McCurley, Sandy Meaut, Toni Payne, Marian Korte Poulos, Sherie Sekul, Syhann Shoemake, Brad Shonk, Ruby Thomas, and Rosella Walker. Thank you for making this project happen.

Charlesbridge and Barbara Barbieri McGrath have arranged to donate 25% of the net proceeds from the sales of this book to Biloxi Public Schools: Biloxi High School, Biloxi Junior High School, Michel Seventh Grade School, Beauvoir Elementary, Gorenflo Elementary, Jeff Davis Elementary, Lopez Elementary, Nichols Elementary, North Bay Elementary, Popp's Ferry Elementary, and the Center for New Opportunities.